U.S. Department of Justice
Office of Justice Programs
Bureau of Justice Statistics

Household Poverty and Nonfatal Violent Victimization, 2008–2012

Erika Harrell, Ph.D., and Lynn Langton, Ph.D., *BJS Statisticians*, Marcus Berzofsky, Dr.P.H., Lance Couzens, and Hope Smiley-McDonald, Ph.D., *RTI International*

For the period 2008–12, persons living in poor households at or below the Federal Poverty Level (FPL) (39.8 per 1,000) had more than double the rate of violent victimization as persons in high-income households (16.9 per 1,000) (figure 1). The percentage of persons reporting violence to police was also higher among households at or below the FPL. More than half of victims of violence from poor households (51%) reported the victimization to police, compared to 45% of victims from high-income households.

This report uses data from the National Crime Victimization Survey (NCVS) to describe the nature of nonfatal violence against persons age 12 or older living in households defined by their percentage above, at, or below the FPL, as measured by the U.S. Department of Health and Human Services (see *Methodology*). The report shows how race and Hispanic origin, location of residence, and poverty are related to violent victimization and the reporting of violent victimization to police. Throughout the report, the terms *at or below the FPL, poor, low income, mid-income,* and *high income* are used to describe household poverty levels. At or below the FPL or poor refers to persons in households at 0% to 100% of the FPL. Low income refers to persons

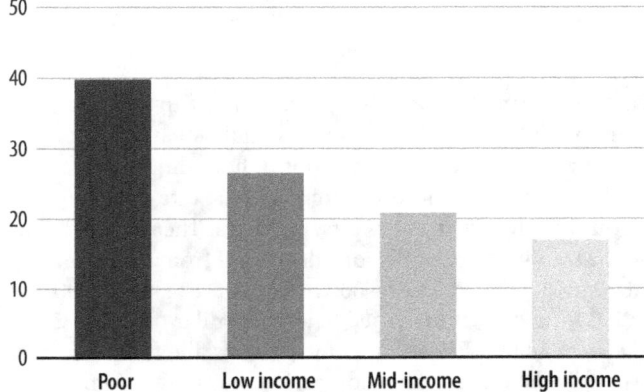

FIGURE 1
Rate of violent victimization, by household poverty level, 2008–2012
Rate per 1,000 persons age 12 or older

Note: Poor refers to households at 0% to 100% of the Federal Poverty Level (FPL). Low income refers to households at 101% to 200% of the FPL. Mid-income refers to households at 201% to 400% of the FPL. High income refers to households at 401% or higher than the FPL. See table 1 for estimates and appendix table 1 for standard errors.
Source: Bureau of Justice Statistics, National Crime Victimization Survey, 2008–2012.

HIGHLIGHTS

This report describes the relationship between nonfatal violent victimization and household poverty level as measured by the U.S. Department of Health and Human Services. Data are from the National Crime Victimization Survey. In 2008–12—

■ Persons in poor households at or below the Federal Poverty Level (FPL) (39.8 per 1,000) had more than double the rate of violent victimization as persons in high-income households (16.9 per 1,000).

■ Persons in poor households had a higher rate of violence involving a firearm (3.5 per 1,000) compared to persons above the FPL (0.8–2.5 per 1,000).

■ The overall pattern of poor persons having the highest rates of violent victimization was consistent for both whites and blacks. However, the rate of violent victimization for Hispanics did not vary across poverty levels.

■ Poor Hispanics (25 3 per 1,000) had lower rates of violence compared to poor whites (46.4 per 1,000) and poor blacks (43.4 per 1,000).

■ Poor persons living in urban areas (43.9 per 1,000) had violent victimization rates similar to poor persons living in rural areas (38.8 per 1,000).

■ Poor urban blacks (51.3 per 1,000) had rates of violence similar to poor urban whites (56.4 per 1,000).

■ Violence against persons in poor (51%) and low-income (50%) households was more likely to be reported to police than violence against persons in mid- (43%) and high-income (45%) households.

in households at 101% to 200% of the FPL. Mid-income refers to persons in households at 201% to 400% of the FPL. High income refers to persons in households at 401% or higher than the FPL. The FPL is generally considered a more robust measure of economic status than income alone because it takes into account the size of the household (see *Methodology*).

The trend estimates presented in this report are based on 2-year rolling averages centered on the most recent year. For example, estimates reported for 2010 represent the average estimates for 2009 and 2010. Other tables focus on the 5-year aggregate period from 2008 through 2012, referred to throughout the report as 2008–12. Both approaches—using rolling averages and aggregating multiple years of data—increase the reliability and stability of estimates and facilitate comparisons of detailed victimization characteristics.

Persons in poor households consistently had the highest rates of violent victimization

Each year from 2009 to 2012, persons living in poor households had a higher rate of nonfatal violent victimization compared to persons in households above the FPL (figure 2). However, trends in the rate of violent victimization varied across poverty levels. The rate of violent victimization for poor persons decreased from 43.1 per 1,000 in 2009 to 34.9 per 1,000 in 2010 and 34.4 per 1,000 in 2011. In 2012, it increased to a rate similar to that in 2009 (41.9 per 1,000). For low-income persons, the rate remained relatively flat during the study period. For mid-income persons, the rate declined slightly from 2009 to 2012. For high-income persons, the rate of violence declined from 2009 (16.2 per 1,000) to 2010 (13.6 per 1,000); by 2012, the rate was higher than it had been in 2009 (19.6 per 1,000).

In 2009, high-income persons had the lowest rate of violent victimization, compared to persons in all other poverty levels. By 2012, mid-income persons (19.1 per 1,000) and high-income persons (19.6 per 1,000) had similar rates of violent victimization—both of which were lower than the rates for low-income persons (27.6 per 1,000) and those at or below the FPL (41.9 per 1,000).

Persons in poor households had more than triple the rate of serious violence compared to persons in high-income households

In 2008–12, the rate of violent victimization was highest for persons in poor households (39.8 per 1,000) and lowest for persons in high-income households (16.9 per 1,000) (table 1). This pattern was consistent across all types of violent crime.

FIGURE 2

Rate of violent victimization, by poverty level, 2009–2012

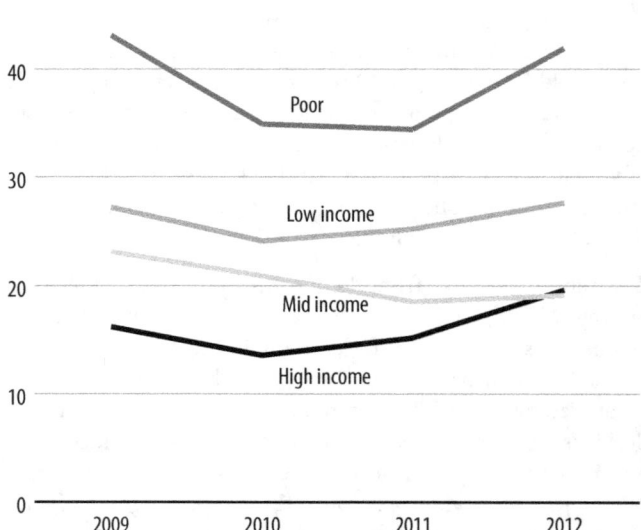

Rate per 1,000 persons age 12 or older

Note: Based on 2-year rolling averages centered on most recent year. Poor refers to households at 0% to 100% of the Federal Poverty Level (FPL). Low income refers to households at 101% to 200% of the FPL. Mid-income refers to households at 201% to 400% of the FPL. High income refers to households at 401% or higher than the FPL. See appendix table 2 for estimates and standard errors.

Source: Bureau of Justice Statistics, National Crime Victimization Survey, 2008–2012.

TABLE 1

Average annual number and rate of violent victimization, by poverty level and type of crime, 2008–2012

Type of crime	All poverty levels		Poor		Low income		Mid-income		High income	
	Number	Rate	Number	Rate	Number	Rate	Number	Rate	Number	Rate
Total violent crime	5,930,800	23.1	1,383,700	39.8	1,385,700	26.5	1,597,800	20.8	1,563,600	16.9
Serious violent crime	1,920,600	7.5	526,900	15.2	467,800	9.0	506,800	6.6	419,100	4.5
Rape/sexual assault	303,000	1.2	75,300	2.2	63,300	1.2	104,800	1.4	59,500	0.6
Robbery	636,500	2.5	190,800	5.5	157,900	3.0	137,100	1.8	150,700	1.6
Aggravated assault	981,100	3.8	260,700	7.5	246,600	4.7	264,900	3.4	208,900	2.3
Simple assault	4,010,200	15.6	856,800	24.7	917,800	17.6	1,091,000	14.2	1,144,600	12.4

Note: Average annual number rounded to the nearest 100. Victimization rates are per 1,000 persons age 12 or older. Poor refers to households at 0% to 100% of the Federal Poverty Level (FPL). Low income refers to households at 101% to 200% of the FPL. Mid-income refers to households at 201% to 400% of the FPL. High income refers to households at 401% or higher than the FPL. See appendix table 1 for standard errors.

Source: Bureau of Justice Statistics, National Crime Victimization Survey, 2008–2012.

Across all poverty levels, serious violence (rape or sexual assault, robbery, and aggravated assault) accounted for less than half of violent victimizations. However, serious violence accounted for a greater percentage of violence among persons in poor households (38%) than those in high-income households (27%) (not shown in table).

Stranger violence was more common for persons living in poor households

In 2008–12, persons in poor households had higher rates of stranger (12.3 per 1,000) and nonstranger (24.2 per 1,000) violence compared to persons at all other poverty levels (table 2). The rate of intimate partner violence for persons in poor households (8.1 per 1,000) was almost double the rate for low-income persons (4.3 per 1,000) and almost four times the rate for high-income persons (2.1 per 1,000).

TABLE 2
Rate of violent victimization, by victim–offender relationship and poverty level, 2008–2012

Victim–offender relationship	All poverty levels	Poor	Low income	Mid-income	High income
Total	23.1	39.8	26.5	20.8	16.9
Nonstranger	12.4	24.2	15.3	10.1	8.1
Intimate partner	3.6	8.1	4.3	2.8	2.1
Other relative	1.6	3.4	2.4	1.2	0.9
Friend/acquaintance	7.1	12.7	8.6	6.1	5.1
Stranger	8.6	12.3	9.1	8.4	7.0
Unknown	1.3	2.2	1.3	1.3	0.9

Note: Victimization rates are per 1,000 persons age 12 or older. Poor refers to households at 0% to 100% of the Federal Poverty Level (FPL). Low income refers to households at 101% to 200% of the FPL. Mid-income refers to households at 201% to 400% of the FPL. High income refers to households at 401% or higher than the FPL. See appendix table 3 for standard errors.

Source: Bureau of Justice Statistics, National Crime Victimization Survey, 2008–2012.

Rates of violent victimization by poverty level and income categories were closely aligned

The main measure of poverty for this report is a household's percentage above, at, or below the Federal Poverty Level (FPL). Prior Bureau of Justice Statistics reports have examined the relationship between annual household income and victimization. However, annual household income may be a misleading indicator of household wealth or poverty because it does not take into account the number of persons in the household. Using annual household income, household size, and the U.S. Federal Poverty Guidelines established by the U.S. Department of Health and Human Services, this report classifies persons according to how their annual household income and household size compare to the FPL (see *Methodology*).

Although poverty level is a more robust measure than income alone, similar patterns in the relationship between wealth and victimization were observed regardless of whether income or poverty was used. Persons in households in the lowest income bracket (less than $15,000) (40.6 per 1,000) and persons in poor households (39.8 per 1,000) had similar rates of violent victimization, and both groups had the highest rates of violent victimization (figure 3). Regardless of the measure used, the rate of violence decreased as households moved above the FPL or income level increased.

FIGURE 3
Rate of violent victimization, by poverty level and annual household income, 2008–2012

Annual household income or poverty level

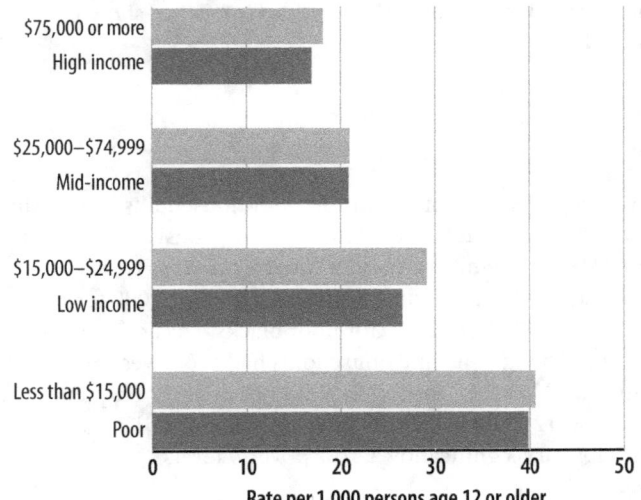

Rate per 1,000 persons age 12 or older

Note: Poor refers to households at 0% to 100% of the Federal Poverty Level (FPL). Low income refers to households at 101% to 200% of the FPL. Mid-income refers to households at 201% to 400% of the FPL. High income refers to households at 401% or higher than the FPL. See appendix table 4 for estimates and standard errors.

Source: Bureau of Justice Statistics, National Crime Victimization Survey, 2008–2012.

Persons in poor and in low-income households had higher rates of violence by nonstrangers than strangers. For persons in these households, about 60% of violent victimizations were committed by someone known to the victim (not shown in table). In comparison, among persons in mid- and high-income households, less than half of victimizations were committed by a nonstranger. Among high-income households, there was no statistically significant difference in the rates of violence by strangers and nonstrangers.

Persons in poor households had the highest rate of violence involving a weapon

In 2008–12, persons in poor households had a higher rate of violent victimization involving a weapon (9.6 per 1,000) and a higher rate of violence involving a firearm (3.5 per 1,000) compared to persons above the FPL (table 3). The rate of violence involving a weapon decreased as households moved away from the FPL. For example, persons in high-income households had the lowest rates of weapon (2.8 per 1,000) and firearm (0.8 per 1,000) violence among all poverty levels.

At each poverty level, the percentage of violence in which the offender had a weapon was lower than the percentage not involving a weapon. However, for persons in poor households, a greater percentage of violent victimizations involved a weapon (24%) compared to the percentage for persons in high-income households (16%) (not shown in table).

Poor whites and blacks had higher rates of violent victimization than poor Hispanics

The overall pattern of persons in poor households having the highest rates of violent victimization was consistent for both non-Hispanic whites and non-Hispanic blacks (figure 4). The rate of violent victimization was 46.4 per 1,000 for poor whites and 43.4 per 1,000 for poor blacks. For both groups, persons in high-income households had the lowest rates of violence. However, this pattern did not hold for Hispanics. In 2008–12, the rate of violent victimization for Hispanics did not vary significantly across poverty levels.

At each of the poverty levels measured, there was no statistically significant difference between whites and blacks in the rate of violent victimization. Among persons in mid- and high-income households, the rates of violence were similar for whites, blacks, and Hispanics. However, poor whites and blacks had higher rates of victimization than poor Hispanics (25.3 per 1,000). Poor Hispanics had similar rates of violence as blacks living in high-income households (22.7 per 1,000).

TABLE 3

Rate of violent victimization, by presence of a weapon and poverty level, 2008–2012

Type of weapon	All poverty levels	Poor	Low income	Mid-income	High income
Total	23.1	39.8	26.5	20.8	16.9
No weapon	16.8	27.2	19.2	15.3	12.8
Weapon	4.7	9.6	5.8	4.1	2.8
Firearm	1.7	3.5	2.5	1.3	0.8
Non-firearm	3.1	6.1	3.3	2.9	1.9
Do not know if weapon present	1.6	3.0	1.5	1.4	1.4

Note: Victimization rates are per 1,000 persons age 12 or older. Poor refers to households at 0% to 100% of the Federal Poverty Level (FPL). Low income refers to households at 101% to 200% of the FPL. Mid-income refers to households at 201% to 400% of the FPL. High income refers to households at 401% or higher than the FPL. See appendix table 5 for standard errors.

Source: Bureau of Justice Statistics, National Crime Victimization Survey, 2008–2012.

FIGURE 4

Rate of violent victimization by poverty level and race or Hispanic origin, 2008–2012

Rate per 1,000 persons age 12 or older

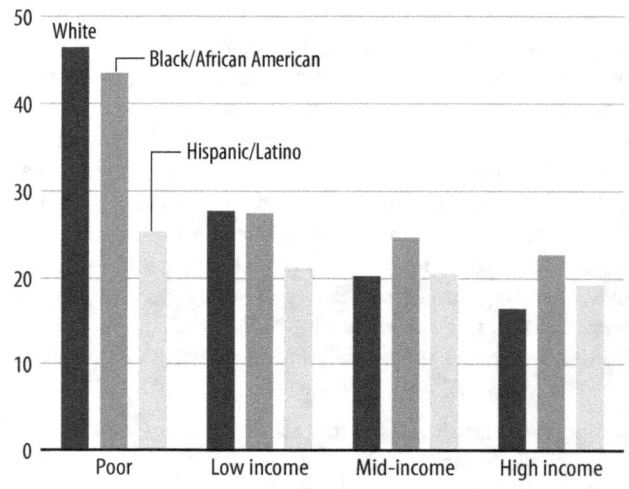

Note: Poor refers to households at 0% to 100% of the Federal Poverty Level (FPL). Low income refers to households at 101% to 200% of the FPL. Mid-income refers to households at 201% to 400% of the FPL. High income refers to households at 401% or higher than the FPL. Excludes persons of Hispanic or Latino origin, unless specified. See appendix table 6 for estimates and standard errors.

Source: Bureau of Justice Statistics, National Crime Victimization Survey, 2008–2012.

Regardless of location of residence, persons in poor households had the highest rates of violent victimization

Regardless of whether households were in urban, suburban, or rural areas, persons in poor households had the highest rates of violence (figure 5). In urban (19.9 per 1,000) and suburban (16.1 per 1,000) areas, persons in high-income households had the lowest rates, while in rural areas, rates were similar for persons in mid- (15.2 per 1,000) and high- (13.3 per 1,000) income households.

Among persons in poor households, the rates of violence were similar in urban (43.9 per 1,000) and rural (38.8 per 1,000) areas. However, among low-, mid-, and high-income households, rates of violent victimization were higher in urban areas than in rural areas. For low- and mid-income households, urban areas had the highest rates of violence. Among high-income households, there was no statistically significant difference in the rates of violence in urban (19.9 per 1,000) and suburban (16.1 per 1,000) areas.

In 2008–12, poor whites (56.4 per 1,000) and poor blacks (51.3 per 1,000) in urban households had higher rates of violence than persons in all other types of households (figure 6). High-income blacks in urban areas (30.1 per 1,000) had similar rates of violence as poor blacks in suburban (35.8 per 1,000) and rural (30.1 per 1,000) households.

FIGURE 5

Rate of violent victimization, by poverty level and location of residence, 2008–2012

Rate per 1,000 persons age 12 or older

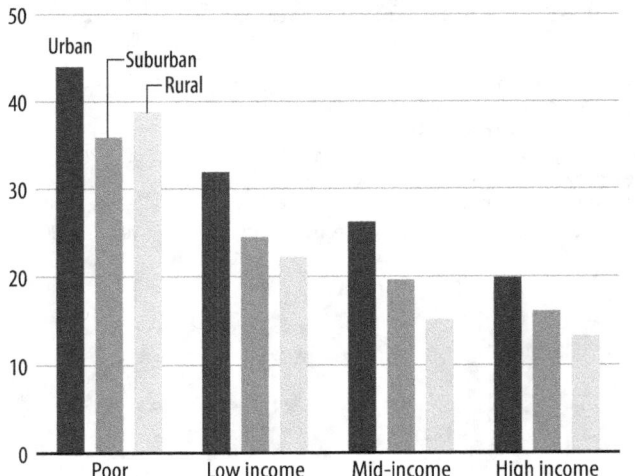

Note: Poor refers to households at 0% to 100% of the Federal Poverty Level (FPL). Low income refers to households at 101% to 200% of the FPL. Mid-income refers to households at 201% to 400% of the FPL. High income refers to households at 401% or higher than the FPL. See appendix table 7 for estimates and standard errors.
Source: Bureau of Justice Statistics, National Crime Victimization Survey, 2008–2012.

FIGURE 6

Rate of violent victimization, by poverty level, race or Hispanic origin, and location of residence, 2008–2012

Rate per 1,000 persons age 12 or older   Urban

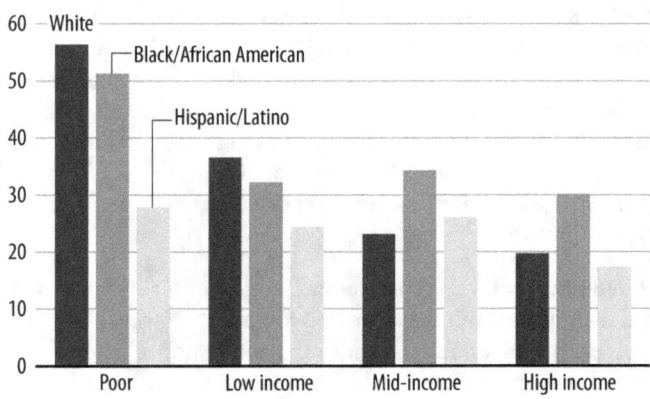

Suburban

Rural

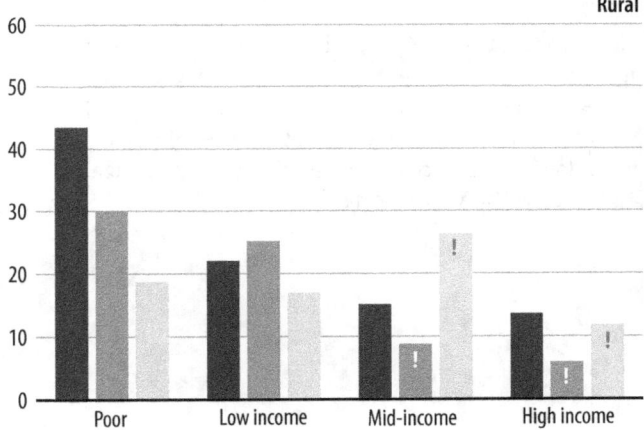

Note: Poor refers to households at 0% to 100% of the Federal Poverty Level (FPL). Low income refers to households at 101% to 200% of the FPL. Mid-income refers to households at 201% to 400% of the FPL. High income refers to households at 401% or higher than the FPL. Excludes persons of Hispanic or Latino origin, unless specified. See appendix table 8 for estimates and standard errors.
! Interpret with caution; estimate based on 10 or fewer sample cases, or coefficient of variation is greater than 50%.
Source: Bureau of Justice Statistics, National Crime Victimization Survey, 2008–2012.

Violence against persons in poor and low-income households was more likely to be reported to police than violence against persons in mid- and high- income households

In 2008–12, about half of violent victimizations against persons in poor households (51%) and in low-income households (50%) were reported to police. In comparison, 43% of victimizations against persons in mid-income households and 45% of victimizations against persons in high-income households were reported (table 4). The percentage of serious violence reported to police did not vary significantly by poverty level.

At all poverty levels, a greater percentage of serious violence than simple assault was reported to police. However, the percentage of serious violence reported to police among persons in mid- (53%) and high- (52%) income households was not significantly different from the percentage of simple assault reported by persons in poor households (46%).

Among blacks, the percentage of violent victimizations reported to police did not vary by poverty level

The pattern of lower reporting of violence among mid- and high-income households held true for whites but not for blacks or Hispanics (figure 7). Among blacks, there was no significant variation across poverty levels in the percentage of violent victimizations reported to police. Among Hispanics, a lower percentage of violence against persons in mid-income households (36%) than those in either poor (50%) or low-income (50%) households was reported to police.

Except for mid-income households, there was no statistically significant difference in the percentage of violence against whites, blacks, and Hispanics reported to police at all poverty levels. Among mid-income households, a higher percentage of violence against blacks (53%) than against Hispanics (36%) was reported to police.

TABLE 4

Violence reported to police, by type of crime and poverty level, 2008–2012

Poverty level	Total violent crime	Serious violent crime	Simple assault
Total	46.9%	55.7%	42.7%
Poor	50.6%	58.2%	45.9%
Low income	50.0	59.1	45.4
Mid-income	43.1	52.8	38.7
High income	44.7	52.3	42.0

Note: Poor refers to households at 0% to 100% of the Federal Poverty Level (FPL). Low income refers to households at 101% to 200% of the FPL. Mid-income refers to households at 201% to 400% of the FPL. High income refers to households at 401% or higher than the FPL. See appendix table 9 for standard errors.

Source: Bureau of Justice Statistics, National Crime Victimization Survey, 2008–2012.

FIGURE 7

Violent victimization reported to police by poverty level and race or Hispanic origin, 2008–2012

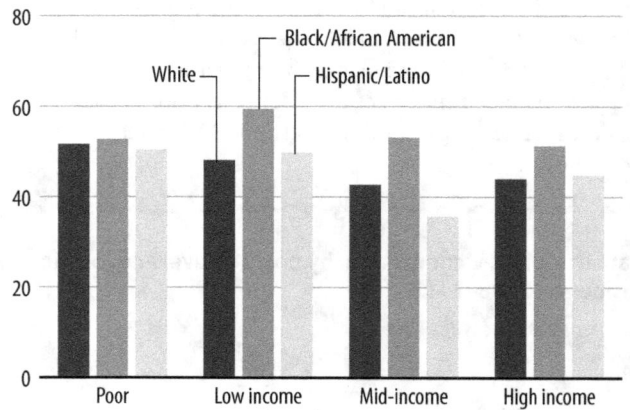

Note: Poor refers to households at 0% to 100% of the Federal Poverty Level (FPL). Low income refers to households at 101% to 200% of the FPL. Mid-income refers to households at 201% to 400% of the FPL. High income refers to households at 401% or higher than the FPL. Excludes persons of Hispanic or Latino origin, unless specified. See appendix table 10 for estimates and standard errors.

Source: Bureau of Justice Statistics, National Crime Victimization Survey, 2008–2012.

The overall pattern of lower reporting among high-income households generally held true in urban areas but not in rural or suburban areas. In urban areas, violence against persons in high-income households (43%) was less likely to be reported to police than violence against persons in households at lower poverty levels (figure 8). In comparison, in rural areas, violence against victims in high-income households (64%) was more likely to be reported to police than violence against those in households at other poverty levels. In suburban areas, there was no statistically significant difference in the percentage of violence reported to police by victims in poor (47%) and high-income (43%) households.

Among persons in poor households and in low- and mid-income households, there was no statistically significant difference in the percentage of violence reported to police in urban, suburban, and rural areas. Among persons in high-income households, the percentage of violence reported to police in rural areas (64%) was higher than the percentage reported in urban (43%) and suburban (43%) areas.

FIGURE 8

Violent victimization reported to police, by poverty level and location of residence, 2008–2012

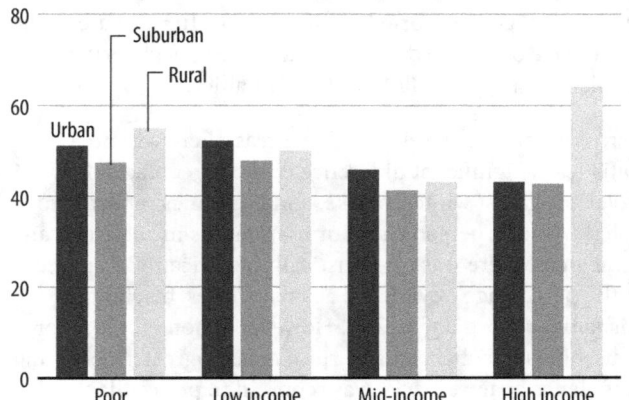

Note: Poor refers to households at 0% to 100% of the Federal Poverty Level (FPL). Low income refers to households at 101% to 200% of the FPL. Mid-income refers to households at 201% to 400% of the FPL. High income refers to households at 401% or higher than the FPL. See appendix table 11 for estimates and standard errors.

Source: Bureau of Justice Statistics, National Crime Victimization Survey, 2008–2012.

Among white and Hispanic households in urban areas, there was no variation in reporting to police across poverty levels (figure 9). However, among black households in urban areas, a lower percentage of violence against persons in high-income households (36%) was reported to police than violence against all other persons. Among black and white suburban households, there was no statistically significant difference between low- and high-income households in the percentage of reported victimizations. In rural areas, the percentage of reported violence varied across poverty levels for blacks and whites but not for Hispanics.

Across all poverty levels in urban areas, there was no statistically significant difference in the percentage of violence against whites, blacks, and Hispanics reported to police. Among persons in poor households in suburban and rural areas, there was no statistically significant difference in the percentage of violence against whites, blacks, and Hispanics reported to police. However, among high-income households in suburban and rural areas, a greater percentage of violence against blacks was reported to police than violence against whites.

FIGURE 9

Violent victimization reported to police, by poverty level, race or Hispanic origin, and location of residence, 2008–2012

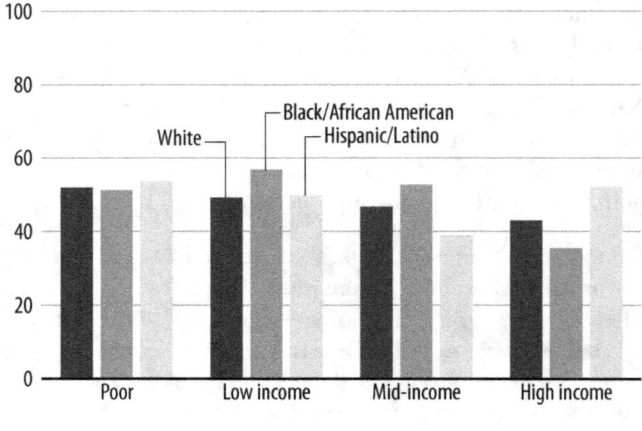

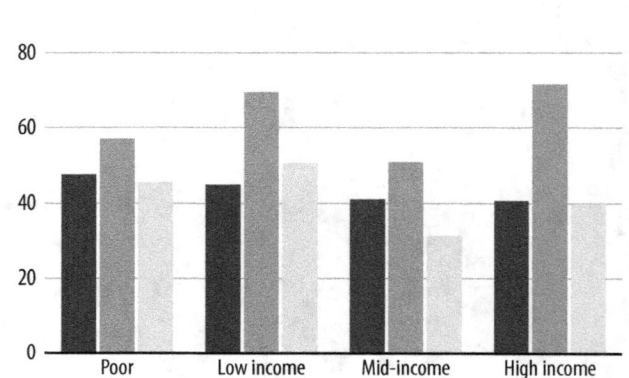

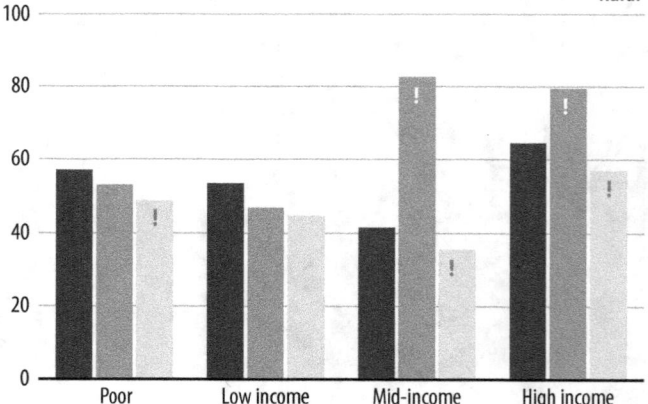

Note: Poor refers to households at 0% to 100% of the Federal Poverty Level (FPL). Low income refers to households at 101% to 200% of the FPL. Mid-income refers to households at 201% to 400% of the FPL. High income refers to households at 401% or higher than the FPL. Excludes persons of Hispanic or Latino origin, unless specified. See appendix table 12 for estimates and standard errors.

! Interpret with caution; estimate based on 10 or fewer sample cases, or coefficient of variation is greater than 50%.

Source: Bureau of Justice Statistics, National Crime Victimization Survey, 2008–2012.

Characteristics of persons in households at each poverty level

In 2008–12, 14% of persons lived in poor households. Based on the Bureau of Justice Statistics' classification, over a third (36%) of persons were in households at 401% or higher than the Federal Poverty Level (FPL), classified as high-income households (table 5).

A greater percentage of females (55%) than males (45%) lived in poor households, and males accounted for half of persons in high-income households (51%). While whites accounted for 68% of all persons nationwide, they were disproportionately represented in high-income households (78%) and underrepresented among poor households (49%). In comparison, blacks and Hispanics accounted for 20% to 25% of persons in poor households, and each accounted for 8% of persons in high-income households.

A greater percentage of persons in poor households (42%) lived in urban areas compared to persons in high-income households (29%). Likewise, a disproportionately high percentage of persons in high-income households resided in suburban areas (59%) compared to the national average (52%). There was little variation across regions of the country in the distribution of persons at different poverty levels.

There was a close relationship between income and poverty as demonstrated by the income distribution of households at different poverty levels. In 2008–12, 73% of persons in poor households had an annual household income of less than $15,000. Among low- (59%) and mid- (88%) income households, the majority of persons fell in the $25,000 to $74,999 income bracket. For high-income households, 80% of persons had a household income of $75,000 or higher.

TABLE 5
Characteristics of persons in households, by poverty level, 2008–2012

Characteristic	Total	Poor	Low income	Mid-income	High income
Total	100%	13.6%	20.4%	30.0%	36.1%
Sex	100%	100%	100%	100%	100%
Male	48.8	45.0	47.0	49.2	50.9
Female	51.2	55.0	53.0	50.8	49.1
Race/Hispanic origin[a]					
White	67.6%	48.6%	57.1%	70.4%	78.2%
Black/African American	11.8	19.7	14.6	11.3	7.8
Hispanic/Latino	14.3	24.7	21.8	12.6	7.6
Other[b]	6.3	7.0	6.5	5.8	6.4
Location of residence					
Urban	32.0%	41.6%	33.7%	29.5%	29.5%
Suburban	51.9	38.5	46.1	53.3	59.2
Rural	16.1	20.0	20.2	17.2	11.4
Region					
Northeast	18.5%	16.2%	15.9%	17.9%	21.4%
Midwest	22.8	22.7	22.7	23.5	22.3
South	35.7	38.9	37.8	35.9	33.2
West	22.9	22.2	23.6	22.7	23.1
Annual household income					
Less than $15,000	11.2%	72.6%	6.7%	--	--
$15,000–$24,999	10.8	22.7	34.1	2.7%	--
$25,000–$74,999	46.1	4.7	59.0	88.0	19.5%
$75,000 or more	31.9	--	--	9.3	80.5

Note: Poor refers to households at 0% to 100% of the Federal Poverty Level (FPL). Low income refers to households at 101% to 200% of the FPL. Mid-income refers to households at 201% to 400% of the FPL. High income refers to households at 401% or higher than the FPL. See appendix table 13 for standard errors. .

[a]Excludes persons of Hispanic or Latino origin, unless specified.

[b]Includes persons identified as American Indian or Alaska Native; Asian, Native Hawaiian, or other Pacific Islander; and persons of two or more races.

--Less than 0.5%.

Source: Bureau of Justice Statistics, National Crime Victimization Survey, 2008–2012.

Methodology

Survey coverage

The National Crime Victimization Survey (NCVS) is an annual data collection conducted by the U.S. Census Bureau for the Bureau of Justice Statistics (BJS). The NCVS is a self-report survey in which interviewed persons are asked about the number and characteristics of victimizations experienced during the prior 6 months. It collects information on nonfatal personal crimes (rape or sexual assault, robbery, aggravated and simple assault, and personal larceny) and household property crimes (burglary, motor vehicle theft, and other theft) both reported and not reported to police. In addition to providing annual level and change estimates on criminal victimization, the NCVS is the primary source of information on the nature of criminal victimization incidents.

Survey respondents provide information about themselves (e.g., age, sex, race and Hispanic origin, marital status, education level, and income) and whether they experienced a victimization. For each victimization incident, the NCVS collects information about the offender (e.g., age, sex, race and Hispanic origin, and victim-offender relationship), characteristics of the crime (including time and place of occurrence, use of weapons, nature of injury, and economic consequences), whether the crime was reported to police, reasons the crime was or was not reported, and victims' experiences with the criminal justice system.

The NCVS is administered to persons age 12 or older from a nationally representative sample of households in the United States. The NCVS defines a household as a group of members who all reside at a sampled address. Persons are considered household members when the sampled address is their usual place of residence at the time of the interview and when they have no usual place of residence elsewhere. Once selected, households remain in the sample for 3 years, and eligible persons in these households are interviewed every 6 months either in person or over the phone for a total of seven interviews.

Generally, all first interviews are conducted in person; subsequent interviews are conducted either in person or by phone. New households rotate into the sample on an ongoing basis to replace outgoing households that have been in the sample for the 3-year period. The sample includes persons living in group quarters, such as dormitories, rooming houses, and religious group dwellings, and excludes persons living in military barracks and institutional settings, such as correctional or hospital facilities, and persons who are homeless.

Nonresponse and weighting adjustments

In 2012, 92,390 households and 162,940 persons age 12 or older were interviewed for the NCVS. Each household was interviewed twice during the year. The response rate was 84% for households and 88% for eligible persons. Victimizations that occurred outside of the United States were excluded from this report. In 2012, less than 1% of the unweighted victimizations occurred outside of the United States and were excluded from the analyses.

Estimates in this report use data from the 2008 to 2012 NCVS data files, weighted to produce annual estimates of victimization for persons age 12 or older living in U.S. households. Because the NCVS relies on a sample rather than a census of the entire U.S. population, weights are designed to inflate sample point estimates to known population totals and to compensate for survey nonresponse and other aspects of the sample design.

NCVS data files include both person and household weights. Person weights provide an estimate of the population represented by each person in the sample. Household weights provide an estimate of the U.S. household population represented by each household in the sample. After proper adjustment, both household and person weights are also typically used to form the denominator in calculations of crime rates.

Victimization weights used in this analysis account for the number of persons present during an incident and for high-frequency repeat victimizations (or series victimizations). Series victimizations are similar in type but occur with such frequency that a victim is unable to recall each individual event or describe each event in detail. Survey procedures allow NCVS interviewers to identify and classify these similar victimizations as series victimizations and to collect detailed information on only the most recent incident in the series.

The weight counts series incidents as the actual number of incidents reported by the victim, up to a maximum of 10 incidents. Including series victimizations in national rates results in large increases in the level of violent victimization; however, trends in violence are generally similar regardless of whether series victimizations are included. In 2012, series incidents accounted for about 1% of all victimizations and 4% of all violent victimizations. Weighting series incidents as the number of incidents up to a maximum of 10 incidents produces more reliable estimates of crime levels, while the cap at 10 minimizes the effect of extreme outliers on the rates. Additional information on the series enumeration is provided in the report *Methods for Counting High-Frequency Repeat Victimizations in the National Crime Victimization Survey* (NCJ 237308, BJS web) April 2012.

Standard error computations

When national estimates are derived from a sample, as with the NCVS, caution must be used when comparing one estimate to another or when comparing estimates over time. Although one estimate may be larger than another, estimates based on a sample have some degree of sampling error. The sampling error of an estimate depends on several factors, including the amount of variation in the responses and the size of the sample. When the sampling error around an estimate is taken into account, the estimates that appear different may not be statistically different.

One measure of the sampling error associated with an estimate is the standard error. The standard error can vary from one estimate to the next. Generally, an estimate with a small standard error provides a more reliable approximation of the true value than an estimate with a large standard error. Estimates with relatively large standard errors are associated with less precision and reliability and should be interpreted with caution.

To generate standard errors around numbers and estimates from the NCVS, Taylor Series Linearization (TSL) was used. TSL is a design-based approach that takes into account aspects of the NCVS complex sample design by specifying the selection method used, the stratification, and the primary sampling units.

Previous NCVS special reports and bulletins relied on a generalized variance function (GVF) provided by the U.S. Census Bureau. A comparison of how TSL performs compared to the GVFs is documented by Williams et al.[1] The comparison shows that TSL estimates of the standard errors provide less variability than the GVF.

BJS conducted tests to determine whether differences in estimated numbers and percentages in this report were statistically significant once sampling error was taken into account. Using statistical programs developed specifically for the NCVS, all comparisons in the text were tested for significance. The primary test procedure used was Student's t-statistic, which tests the difference between two sample estimates. To ensure that the observed differences between estimates were larger than might be expected due to sampling variation, the significance level was set at the 95% confidence level in most cases. In a few instances, the significance level was set at 90%. Caution must be taken when comparing estimates not explicitly discussed in this report.

Data users can use the estimates and the standard errors of the estimates provided in this report to generate a confidence interval around each estimate as a measure of the margin of error. The following example illustrates how standard errors can be used to generate confidence intervals:

---

[1] Williams, R., Heller, D., Couzens, L., Shook-Sa, B., Berzofsky, M., Smiley-McDonald, H. & Krebs, C. (In press). *Evaluation of Direct Variance Estimation, Estimate Reliability and Confidence Intervals for the National Crime Victimization Survey.*

In 2008–12, there were 24.2 violent victimizations per 1,000 persons committed by a nonstranger among persons in poor households (see table 2). Using TSL, BJS determined that the estimate has a standard error of 1.6 violent victimizations per 1,000 persons (see appendix table 3). A confidence interval around the estimate was generated by multiplying the standard errors by ±1.96 (the t-score of a normal, two-tailed distribution that excludes 2.5% at either end of the distribution). Thus, the confidence interval around the 24.2 violent victimizations per 1,000 persons estimate is equal to 24.2 ± 1.6 X 1.96 (or 21.1 violent victimizations per 1,000 persons to 27.3 violent victimizations per 1,000 persons). In other words, if different samples using the same procedures were taken from the U.S. population in 2008–12, 95% of the time the rate of violent victimizations committed by a nonstranger among persons in poor households would fall between 21.1 and 27.3.

In this report, BJS also calculated a coefficient of variation (CV) for all estimates, representing the ratio of the standard error to the estimate. CVs provide a measure of reliability and a means for comparing the precision of estimates across measures with differing levels or metrics. In cases where the CV was greater than 50%, or the unweighted sample had 10 or fewer cases, the estimate was noted with a "!" symbol (interpret data with caution; estimate is based on 10 or fewer sample cases, or coefficient of variation exceeds 50%).

Many of the variables examined in this report may be related to one another and to other variables not included in the analyses. Complex relationships among variables in this report were not fully explored and warrant more extensive analysis. Readers are cautioned not to draw causal inferences based on the results presented.

Measuring household income as a percentage of the Federal Poverty Level

The main measure of poverty for this report is household income as a percentage above, at, or below the Federal Poverty Level (FPL). The NCVS asks the reference person of a household about the household's income level during the first interview and every odd-numbered interview after that. When household income is not asked, the income from the previous interview is carried forward. When included, respondents are asked to choose a household income from 1 of 14 categories (the highest category is an income of $75,000 or more).

A household's income may be a misleading indicator of a household's wealth because it does not take into account the number of persons in the household. A household's income as it relates to the poverty level is a better measure of overall wealth because it takes into account family size. In the United States, poverty is defined by one of two measures: the poverty threshold and the poverty guideline. The *poverty threshold* is defined by the U.S. Census Bureau and is used for all statistical measures of poverty in the United States. It is the same in all 50 states and varies by family size, number of children, number of adults (one or two), and whether the reference person in the household is elderly.

The *poverty guideline* is defined by the U.S. Department of Health and Human Services (DHHS) and is used to determine eligibility for many federal and state programs. It is defined the same for the contiguous 48 states and Washington, DC, but is different in Alaska and Hawaii and varies by family size. Both measures change each year as dictated by the federal agency that oversees them. More information on the two measures and how they differ can be found here: http://aspe.hhs.gov/poverty/14poverty.cfm.

The measure used by the NCVS is the poverty guideline. The poverty guideline can be operationalized more easily than the poverty threshold and it is commonly referred to as the Federal Poverty Level (or FPL). While the poverty threshold is used for official statistics from the U.S. Census Bureau, given the information on household composition available in the NCVS, it is more cumbersome to implement. Furthermore, an analysis of the two measures found that a household's resulting percentage of the FPL did not vary much between the two measures. One drawback to the poverty guideline is that it is different in Alaska and Hawaii relative to the rest of the United States and households in these two states cannot be identified on the NCVS public use file. Therefore, households in these two states may not have a proper percentage of the FPL assigned. However, the number of households in the NCVS sample in these two states is small. As a result, the impact of not differentiating the poverty level in these states is negligible.

To determine a household's income as a percentage of the FPL, two pieces of information are needed: a household's income and the number of people in the household.

Determining a household's income

As described earlier, a question about household income is asked during every other interview and households are asked to indicate a range for their income rather than a specific amount. These procedures are intended to minimize the burden and intrusiveness respondents may feel about providing their income. However, even with these procedures, an average of 31% of households during the study period of 2008–12 (a range between 28.4% and 32.4%) did not provide a household income when asked. To effectively analyze criminal victimization by poverty status, household income needed to be imputed when a household did not provide a value. As detailed in Berzofsky et al., a household's missing income category was imputed using a hot deck approach that relied on one of two methods, depending on the household's previous income response status.[2] When a household provided a household income category in a previous interview, the previous income value was used to predict the household's current income level. When a household had never provided a household income value, the distribution of household income among respondents from the interview period of interest was used to predict the household's current income level. Because these procedures require linking households across their interview waves, the imputation process could only be implemented starting in 2008. In 2006, the scrambled control numbers the U.S. Census Bureau uses to identify households were changed to account for the phase-in of the 2000 Census primary sampling units. Therefore, 2007 was used as a base year from which households in existing sample rotation groups could be linked in 2008 and beyond.

Even with a household income assigned to all respondents, the income categories used in the NCVS do not map well to percentages of the FPL for two primary reasons. The FPL changes each year based on the DHHS recommendations, while the NCVS income categories are fixed and are the same each year. In addition, the FPL varies based on the number of persons in the household, while the NCVS household income categories are the same regardless of the number of persons in the household. Therefore, to determine a household's income as a percentage of the FPL, a precise income dollar amount needs to be interpolated based on a household's assigned income category. This process was done in four broad steps:

1. *Stratification classes were formed based on characteristics highly correlated to a household's income.* For this analysis period, a household reference person's race and age categories were used to form income stratification classes.

2. *The distribution of income was determined within each stratum.* Using the cumulative distribution of the income categories and assuming a log-normal distribution, a grid search was used to find the optimal mean and standard deviation for income across all persons in the specified stratum.

3. *The range for each income category was determined.* For a particular stratum and income category, using the log-normal distribution, the percentile range between the upper and lower bound for a category was determined.

---

[2] Berzofsky, M., Smiley-McDonald, H., Moore, A. & Krebs, C. (In press). *Measuring Socioeconomic Status (SES) in the NCVS: Background, Options and Recommendations.*

4. *An interpolated income value was assigned to each household.* Given an optimal log-normal distribution and the inter-percentile range for an income category in which a household resides, and using a random uniform variate between the upper and lower bounds, an interpolated log-income value was selected. The exponentiated log-income value was the interpolated income for a household.

Determining a household's income as a percentage of the FPL

Using the interpolated household income and the number of persons in the household, the percentage of the FPL for the household was calculated as—

$$PCT\_FPL = \frac{HH\_INC}{FPL_{yi}} \times 100$$

where FPL_{yi} was the FPL in year y for i persons living in the household.

Validating method for determining the percentage of the FPL

After applying the above-described procedures to assign each household a percentage of the FPL value, the distribution of the percentage of the FPL was validated to ensure that the distribution used in this analysis comported with other federal benchmark surveys. The Current Population Survey's Annual Social and Economic Supplement (CPS-ASEC) provided a benchmark estimate of the distribution of a household's percentage of the FPL for all persons, including by the race or ethnicity category (see table number POV05 on https://www.census.gov/hhes/www/poverty/data/incpovhlth/2012/index.html). The validation process found that for all years from 2008 to 2012, the overall distribution of the percentage of the FPL in the NCVS and the distributions for all race or ethnicity categories (i.e., non-Hispanic white, non-Hispanic black, Hispanic, and non-Hispanic Asian) were similar to the distribution found in the CPS-ASEC.

Standard errors for table 1: Average annual number and rate of violent victimization, by poverty level and type of crime, 2008–2012

Type of crime	All poverty levels		Poor		Low income		Mid-income		High income	
	Number	Rate	Number	Rate	Number	Rate	Number	Rate	Number	Rate
Total violent crime	208,600	0.7	77,400	2.1	73,600	1.3	83,400	1.0	84,100	0.8
Serious violent crime	82,500	0.3	38,500	1.1	29,500	0.5	40,500	0.5	32,100	0.3
Rape/sexual assault	38,800	0.1	10,900	0.3	13,200	0.2	24,300	0.3	13,400	0.1
Robbery	40,600	0.2	19,200	0.5	12,600	0.2	16,500	0.2	20,400	0.2
Aggravated assault	42,200	0.2	23,400	0.7	20,500	0.4	21,800	0.3	18,700	0.2
Simple assault	162,600	0.6	54,000	1.5	59,800	1.1	66,100	0.8	74,900	0.8

Source: Bureau of Justice Statistics, National Crime Victimization Survey, 2008–2012.

Estimates and standard errors for figure 2: Rate of violent victimization, by poverty level, 2009–2012

Year	Poor		Low income		Mid-income		High income	
	Estimate	Standard error	Estimate	Standard error	Estimate	Standard error	Estimate	Standard error
2009	43.1	3.6	27.2	1.9	23.1	1.7	16.2	1.0
2010	34.9	2.9	24.1	1.9	20.9	1.8	13.6	1.1
2011	34.4	2.2	25.2	1.8	18.5	1.4	15.2	1.4
2012	41.9	2.6	27.6	1.8	19.1	1.2	19.6	1.7

Source: Bureau of Justice Statistics, National Crime Victimization Survey, 2008–2012.

Standard errors for table 2: Rate of violent victimization, by victim–offender relationship and poverty level, 2008–2012

Victim-offender relationship	All poverty levels	Poor	Low income	Mid income	High income
Total	0.7	2.1	1.3	1.0	0.8
Nonstranger	0.5	1.6	1.0	0.7	0.6
Intimate partner	0.2	0.9	0.5	0.4	0.3
Other relative	0.1	0.5	0.4	0.2	0.2
Friend/acquaintance	0.4	1.0	0.7	0.5	0.5
Stranger	0.3	0.9	0.6	0.6	0.5
Unknown	0.1	0.3	0.2	0.2	0.2

Source: Bureau of Justice Statistics, National Crime Victimization Survey, 2008–2012.

Standard errors for table 3: Rate of violent victimization, by presence of a weapon and poverty level, 2008–2012

Type of weapon	All poverty levels	Poor	Low income	Mid- income	High income
Total	0.7	2.1	1.3	1.0	0.8
No weapon	0.6	1.5	1.1	0.9	0.8
Weapon	0.2	0.8	0.4	0.3	0.2
Firearm	0.1	0.5	0.3	0.1	0.1
Non-firearm	0.2	0.6	0.3	0.3	0.2
Do not know if weapon present	0.1	0.5	0.2	0.2	0.2

Source: Bureau of Justice Statistics, National Crime Victimization Survey, 2008–2012.

Estimates and standard errors for figure 3: Rate of violent victimization, by poverty level and annual household income, 2008–2012

Characteristic	Estimate	Standard error
Annual household income		
Less than $15,000	40.6	2.2
$15,000–$24,999	29.1	1.8
$25,000–$74,999	20.9	0.9
$75,000 or more	18.1	1.0
Poverty level		
Poor	39.8	2.1
Low income	26.5	1.3
Mid-income	20.8	1.0
High income	16.9	0.8

Source: Bureau of Justice Statistics, National Crime Victimization Survey, 2008–2012.

APPENDIX TABLE 6
Estimates and standard errors for figure 4: Rate of violent victimization, by poverty level and race or Hispanic origin, 2008–2012

Race/Hispanic origin	Poor		Low income		Mid-income		High income	
	Estimate	Standard error	Estimate	Standard error	Estimate	Standard error	Estimate	Standard error
White	46.4	3.2	27.7	1.8	20.3	1.2	16.4	0.9
Black/African American	43.4	3.8	27.5	2.6	24.7	2.9	22.7	5.1
Hispanic/Latino	25.3	2.6	21.2	1.9	20.6	2.4	19.3	3.4

Source: Bureau of Justice Statistics, National Crime Victimization Survey, 2008–2012.

APPENDIX TABLE 7
Estimates and standard errors for figure 5: Rate of violent victimization, by poverty level and location of residence, 2008–2012

Location of residence	Poor		Low income		Mid-income		High income	
	Estimate	Standard error	Estimate	Standard error	Estimate	Standard error	Estimate	Standard error
Urban	43.9	2.8	31.9	1.9	26.2	1.9	19.9	1.5
Suburban	35.9	3.4	24.5	2.0	19.6	1.4	16.1	1.2
Rural	38.8	3.9	22.2	2.9	15.2	1.7	13.3	2.2

Source: Bureau of Justice Statistics, National Crime Victimization Survey, 2008–2012.

APPENDIX TABLE 8
Estimates and standard errors for figure 6: Rate of violent victimization, by poverty level, race or Hispanic origin, and location of residence, 2008–2012

Location of residence	Poor		Low income		Mid-income		High income	
	Estimate	Standard error	Estimate	Standard error	Estimate	Standard error	Estimate	Standard error
Urban								
White	56.4	5.3	36.6	3.7	23.1	1.8	19.7	1.8
Black/African American	51.3	5.5	32.2	3.7	34.3	5.3	30.1	6.8
Hispanic/Latino	27.8	3.8	24.4	2.9	26.1	4.4	17.3	2.3
Suburban								
White	41.4	4.7	26.7	2.7	21.0	1.8	15.7	1.1
Black/African American	35.8	6.9	21.9	3.5	18.0	3.1	18.8	8.4
Hispanic/Latino	23.7	3.6	18.7	3.0	15.5	2.6	21.4	6.0
Rural								
White	43.5	5.5	22.1	3.4	15.1	1.9	13.6	2.4
Black/African American	30.1	5.9	25.2	7.9	8.8 !	3.8	5.9 !	2.9
Hispanic/Latino	18.7	3.0	16.9	3.6	26.3 !	14.2	11.8 !	5.8

! Interpret with caution; estimate based on 10 or fewer sample cases, or coefficient of variation is greater than 50%.
Source: Bureau of Justice Statistics, National Crime Victimization Survey, 2008–2012.

APPENDIX TABLE 9
Standard errors for table 4: Violence reported to police, by type of crime and poverty level, 2008–2012

Poverty level	Total violent crime	Serious violent crime	Simple assault
Total	1.1%	1.6%	1.4%
Poor	2.0%	3.0%	2.5%
Low income	2.1	2.9	2.6
Mid-income	1.8	3.4	2.4
High income	2.3	3.5	3.0

Source: Bureau of Justice Statistics, National Crime Victimization Survey, 2008–2012.

Estimates and standard errors for figure 7: Violent victimization reported to police, by poverty level and race or Hispanic origin, 2008–2012

Race/Hispanic origin	Poor		Low income		Mid-income		High income	
	Estimate	Standard error	Estimate	Standard error	Estimate	Standard error	Estimate	Standard error
White	51.7%	3.1%	48.1%	2.9%	42.7%	2.4%	44.0%	2.4%
Black/African American	52.8	3.5	59.4	4.9	53.2	4.8	51.3	11.8
Hispanic/Latino	50.4	4.9	49.8	4.2	35.7	4.6	44.8	8.3

Source: Bureau of Justice Statistics, National Crime Victimization Survey, 2008–2012.

Estimates and standard errors for figure 8: Violent victimization reported to police, by poverty level and location of residence, 2008–2012

Location of residence	Poor		Low income		Mid-income		High income	
	Estimate	Standard error	Estimate	Standard error	Estimate	Standard error	Estimate	Standard error
Urban	51.2%	2.6%	52.3%	3.0%	45.8%	3.0%	43.1%	3.2%
Suburban	47.4	4.1	47.8	3.1	41.2	2.8	42.7	3.3
Rural	55.0	4.2	50.1	5.8	43.0	4.7	64.0	5.1

Source: Bureau of Justice Statistics, National Crime Victimization Survey, 2008–2012.

Estimates and standard errors for figure 9: Violent victimization reported to police, by poverty level, race or Hispanic origin, and location of residence, 2008–2012

Location of residence	Poor		Low income		Mid-income		High income	
	Estimate	Standard error	Estimate	Standard error	Estimate	Standard error	Estimate	Standard error
Urban								
White	51.9%	4.3%	49.2%	4.7%	46.7%	3.7%	43.0%	4.0%
Black/African American	51.2	4.0	56.8	6.3	52.7	6.3	35.5	8.7
Hispanic/Latino	53.7	6.9	49.8	5.8	39.0	7.2	52.1	5.3
Suburban								
White	47.6%	5.4%	44.9%	3.8%	41.1%	3.5%	40.7%	3.3%
Black/African American	57.0	9.5	69.6	6.6	50.8	8.7	71.7	15.1
Hispanic/Latino	45.5	7.0	50.6	6.3	31.3	5.5	39.9	12.3
Rural								
White	57.0%	5.1%	53.4%	7.0%	41.6%	5.0%	64.5%	5.7%
Black/African American	53.0	9.0	46.8	15.5	82.6 !	12.1	79.4 !	19.1
Hispanic/Latino	48.7 !	11.2	44.7	10.3	35.6 !	10.9	56.9 !	17.8

! Interpret with caution; estimate based on 10 or fewer sample cases, or coefficient of variation is greater than 50%.

Source: Bureau of Justice Statistics, National Crime Victimization Survey, 2008–2012.

Standard errors for table 5: Characteristics of persons in households, by poverty level, 2008–2012

Characteristic	Total	Poor	Low income	Mid-income	High income
Total	--	0.2%	0.2%	0.2%	0.3%
Sex					
Male	0.1%	0.3%	0.2%	0.1%	0.1%
Female	0.1	0.3	0.2	0.1	0.1
Race/Hispanic origin					
White	0.6%	1.0%	0.8%	0.6%	0.4%
Black/African American	0.4	0.9	0.6	0.4	0.3
Hispanic/Latino	0.5	1.0	0.7	0.5	0.2
Other	0.2	0.4	0.3	0.2	0.2
Location of residence					
Urban	0.9%	1.3%	1.0%	0.9%	0.8%
Suburban	1.1	1.3	1.3	1.2	1.0
Rural	1.3	1.7	1.6	1.4	1.0
Region					
Northeast	0.4%	0.6%	0.4%	0.4%	0.5%
Midwest	0.5	0.7	0.6	0.6	0.7
South	0.5	0.8	0.7	0.6	0.6
West	0.6	0.8	0.8	0.7	0.6
Annual household income					
Less than $15,000	0.2%	0.5%	0.2%	--	--
$15,000–$24,999	0.1	0.4	0.4	0.1%	--
$25,000–$74,999	0.3	0.2	0.4	0.2	0.2%
$75,000 or more	0.3	--	--	0.2	0.2

--Less than 0.5%.

Source: Bureau of Justice Statistics, National Crime Victimization Survey, 2008–2012.

www.ingramcontent.com/pod-product-compliance
Lightning Source LLC
Chambersburg PA
CBHW081144280526
45787CB00007B/3217